Original title:
A House of Love and Memories

Copyright © 2025 Creative Arts Management OÜ
All rights reserved.

Author: Rosalie Bradford
ISBN HARDBACK: 978-1-80587-141-5
ISBN PAPERBACK: 978-1-80587-611-3

Woven Memories

In the attic, old socks lie,
With dust bunnies playing nearby.
A cat sits, eyeing the mouse,
Who's taken up residence in the house.

Grandma's laughter fills the air,
As she tells stories without a care.
The dog barks, chasing shadows,
While baby siblings nap, nose to nose.

A family photo—oh, what a sight!
Dad's hairstyle could give you a fright.
Mom's apron's from a wild baking spree,
And we all laugh till we cry, oh me!

They say time flies, but here it crawls,
With mismatched socks and echoing brawls.
Yet in every giggle, there's a trace,
Of the love that made this our favorite space.

A Tapestry of Time

The kitchen's fragrant with burnt toast,
Dad just finished with his grand roast.
We all grimace at the smoke-filled air,
But oh, the stories it will share!

The living room's cluttered with toys,
Each corner filled with loud, happy noise.
A pillow fight starts with a giggle,
As Dad yells, 'Stop it!' then joins the wiggle.

Cousins spin tales of ghostly fright,
Under blankets with squeals in the night.
While Uncle Joe's snoring is loud as a train,
We all wonder if he'll ever regain.

Still, through the chaos, joy floats around,
With each silly moment, forever bound.
A patchwork quilt, with memories sewn,
In this quirky shelter, we've truly grown.

Remnants of Warm Smiles

In the corners, laughter hides,
With echoes of our silly rides.
A pillow fort from yesterday,
Where giggles linger and sunbeams play.

The fridge adorned with sticky notes,
From past adventures and silly quotes.
A mix of memories and tasty treats,
Silly sketches, and tiny feats.

Treasures in the Closet

In dusty corners, treasures wait,
A polka-dot dress, a tale of fate.
Old shoes that danced a thousand times,
Whispers of youth in joyful rhymes.

A box of cards from years ago,
Laughs and tears, an ageless show.
Each find a quirk of joyful past,
Reminding us how moments last.

Chasing Sunbeams

Through the windows, sunbeams bounce,
As shadows waltz and giggles flounce.
On lazy days, we chase the light,
In games of tag till stars are bright.

With ice cream drips and joyful squeals,
We build with laughter, stack our feels.
A net of dreams, we toss and weave,
In every corner, magic we believe.

The Embrace of Silence

In quiet nooks, the silence sings,
Of whispered dreams and secret things.
A comfy chair, where thoughts take flight,
With chuckles waiting to ignite.

The clock ticks softly, time slows down,
A cozy pause while wearing crowns.
In jigsaw puzzles of tangled fun,
We find our peace when day is done.

A Portrait of Stillness

In the corner stands a cat,
A fuzzy diplomat,
He rules the room with silent glares,
While plotting snags in comfy chairs.

Old photos stare from dusty walls,
With hats too big and silly sprawls.
The laughter trapped in frame and time,
Echoes softly in rhyme and mime.

The creaky floorboards play along,
Each step a note in the silly song.
Grandma's tea is always cold,
But her stories still stay bold.

And through it all, the memories dance,
In every glance, a tale, a chance.
We laugh at how we once wore socks,
That stretched like time on ticking clocks.

The Silence that Speaks

The refrigerator hums a tune,
A somber serenade to the moon.
It whispers secrets of leftovers past,
A curry that didn't quite last.

The couch is a time machine of sorts,
It swallows socks and old sports shorts.
A drink spilled here, a crumb over there,
The laughter lingers in the air.

Light bulbs flicker like a disco scene,
From a party that never could have been.
The silence holds its subtle puns,
As dust bunnies play with forgotten runs.

And when the wind nudges the door,
We hear echoes of friends who swore,
To come back, but they lost their map,
And now it's just us in this cozy trap.

Echoing Moments

A chair that squeaks a tune of glee,
Where stories brew like endless tea.
It bounces back with each retold,
Of pets who dared to be too bold.

The table groans beneath the weight,
Of birthday cakes and a sad old fate.
It still remembers the frosting fights,
And laughter that stretched through silly nights.

The windows rattle with a chuckle low,
As breezes carry the tales we know.
Each gust a giggle, each creak a jest,
In this joyful mess, we are blessed.

Let's raise a glass to daft delight,
To memories shimmering in soft light.
Each echo sings of moments dear,
In the walls that hold our laughter near.

The Stairs of Remembrance

Up and down the stairs we tread,
Each step whispers of crumbs and bread.
They squeak in rhythm, a dance so sweet,
A reminder of errant tiny feet.

With every stumble, a tale unfurls,
Of falling down and dizzy swirls.
The banister knows our secret spills,
Of laughter shared and tiny thrills.

In sock wars fought with reckless glee,
Each landing holds a memory.
Of sleepy heads and pillow fights,
Captured in those starry nights.

So let us climb these steps once more,
Revisit dreams that we adore.
For every creak helps us reflect,
On love and joy we can't neglect.

Unspoken Bonds

In the corner, a sock awaits,
It's lost its partner, oh what fates!
Under the couch, crumbs remain,
Each a memory, joy and pain.

Laughter echoes, a distant bell,
As the dog chases its own tail.
Remember the time we tried to cook?
The smoke alarm gave us quite the look!

Mismatched chairs and giggling kids,
Who knew chaos could hold such bids?
A broomstick horse, our wildest ride,
Together we conquered, side by side.

With food fights and silly dances,
Each moment brings us strange romances.
This quirky abode, a treasure chest,
Where silly hearts weave their best jest.

Overhead Dreams

Up on the shelf, a dust bunny reigns,
With dreams of conquering wasteful stains.
A lost toy soldier, with paint a-peeling,
Claims victory over a peanut ceiling.

The ceiling fan whirls with mighty grace,
As we perfect our dance in this space.
Who knew that upside-down could be fun?
While we twist and twirl till the day is done!

Rainy days call for indoor fun,
Building forts until the day is done.
Socks for curtains, chairs for walls,
Laughter erupts as the fortress falls.

And when night falls, we share our dreams,
Tales of adventures, of wild extremes.
Beneath this roof, our spirits soar,
Reminiscing how we grew, and more!

Love Letters in the Attic

In the attic lies a box so grand,
With scribbled notes from our young hands.
'You're a banana!' one note dared say,
Imagining love in the funniest way.

Mismatched earrings and shoes askew,
Remind us of dance-offs with our crew.
The love letters passed during class,
'You're cute, but your lunch looks like grass!'

A teddy bear with one button eye,
Whispers to us as we float by.
Dreams of picnics and secret plans,
Lending smiles with those little hands.

So here we sit, amidst dusty things,
Sharing our joy, the laughter it brings.
For each odd trinket holds a tale,
Of wild adventures that never fail.

Reflections in the Window

Through the window, we see our past,
As the neighbor's cat thinks it's a blast.
Peering in, the view's a delight,
With mismatched socks in a playful fight.

The old swing creaks, a favorite place,
Where giggles chase the wind's wild race.
Above, a bird mocks our every chat,
'The food smells funny, do you smell that?'

Through reflection, we see our youth,
A snapshot of chaos with a bit of truth.
Each tear and laugh, a colorful thread,
Woven tightly into the life we've led.

So here's to the dances and silly pranks,
To all our messy, delightful flanks.
In every reflection, lies our glee,
As we laugh at the roots of old family trees.

Memories Wrapped in Fabric

In the closet, shirts collide,
Old socks giggle, hope they hide.
A sweater shrieks, "I was the best!"
As dust bunnies throw a fabric fest.

Pajamas whisper bedtime tales,
While curtains plot their daring gales.
A blanket sighs, "I was so warm!"
That throw pillow's hiding a rumor storm!

Forgotten scarves parade in line,
Chasing laughter, oh so fine.
Each fabric has its own sweet song,
In this jumble, we belong.

Tangled yarn speaks of late-night chats,
While a patchwork quilt hides silly flats.
In cozy chaos, we find the cheer,
With every stitch, our hearts draw near.

The Nest of Our Journey

In the corner, there's a big old chair,
Where cats plot world domination, I swear.
It creaks and groans as we sink down,
Like two old souls in a thrift shop gown.

The kitchen's a kitchen dance-floor zone,
Where I step on toes, but not my own.
Pasta flings, and laughter flies,
Even the noodles share secret sighs.

Candles flicker with jokes untold,
Lighting up moments, both shy and bold.
The fridge hums sweet serenades at night,
While leftovers plot to take flight!

Outside, the garden's a riot of sun,
Where weeds and daisies have a good run.
A swing set squeaks with joy and delight,
In this nest, our dreams take flight.

Treasure Boxes of Time

In the attic, boxes stack up high,
Each one whispers, "Come give a try!"
A teddy bear tells tales of glee,
While old board games plot a victory spree.

Albums with pictures from days gone by,
Smile at us with a twinkling eye.
A shoebox of ticket stubs and notes,
Reminds us of youth and crazy quotes.

A vase, once chipped, stands proud and tall,
With dried flowers, a memory wall.
Each item holds a giggly past,
In this treasure, our hearts are cast.

Dust motes dance as we sift through years,
Laughter mingles with joyful tears.
These boxes are time machines, you see,
Where silly moments feel wild and free.

Lyrics of the Heart

In the living room, music's a blast,
A playlist of loves from the distant past.
Where the vacuum's a bandmate on Tuesdays,
And dance-offs are mandatory in all ways!

The cat's the DJ, with paws on the turn,
Purring out beats as we twirl and churn.
A spatula sings a frying pan tune,
While the fridge joins in, harmonizing soon.

Forgotten classics and off-key notes,
Celebrate moments we both wrote.
With laughter the lyrics, we change every time,
In this comical concert, a rhythm and rhyme.

We steal the spotlight, just two goofy stars,
Plucking heartstrings in our funny car.
With every chorus, we build a new part,
In this melody of joy, we find our heart.

Threads of Our Tapestry.

In the corner hangs a sweater,
Knit by Auntie with much care.
It wobbled off into the cat,
Now it's a very stylish chair.

A quilt crafted from old T-shirts,
With faces of legends from the past.
Each patch holds a wild story,
Like Grandpa's botched magic cast.

The curtains dance with laughter,
As Grandma's recipes float by.
Mixing love with a pinch of sauce,
And the occasional pineapple pie.

Our laughter stitched through time,
With buttons that never quite fit.
In this wild, patchwork family,
Fumbles lead to the best bit.

Whispers in the Attic

Up in the attic, shadows play,
With board games long left behind.
An old doll whispers secrets,
Of adventures we never designed.

In the box lies our childhood,
With crayons melted together.
Sketches of everyone we loved,
And the dog in a green sweater.

A trumpet from a school band,
That never quite hit the note.
The cat thought it a mountain,
And claimed it as his remote.

Each corner a patch of laughter,
Echoes of hilarity remain.
In dust, we find our treasures,
And jumped back to joy like a train.

Echoes of Laughter

In the garden, we set up camp,
With tea made of daisies and hope.
We tried to catch a sneaky squirrel,
Who stole our last slice of soap.

The pool noodle stuck as a sword,
Battling pirates in the sun.
But someone slipped on the grass,
And now it's a hero's run!

Echoes of giggles linger,
As we take turns on the swing.
An octopus made of pool floats,
Proudly reigns as our king.

Flares of joy in the twilight,
Photos capturing our cheer.
Each snapshot holds a story,
Of all the fun we hold dear.

Portraits of Yesterday

The old fridge hums a soft tune,
As leftovers fight for their place.
Mom's casserole losing the battle,
Duck sauce dripped all over the face.

Above hangs a portrait of Dad,
Wearing an outrageous hat.
He claims it was haute couture,
We just call it a comical spat.

Siblings pose in worn-out jeans,
Caught in a tickle attack.
With laughter spilling like jelly,
And dreams of a snack back-to-back.

Even the dog made the frame,
Grinning with breakfast crumbs near.
In this gallery of memories,
The art is a feast for good cheer.

Sighs Beneath the Eaves

In the attic I found a hat,
It belonged to my old cat.
Wearing it felt quite absurd,
Even she thought it was a bird.

Ghosts of laughter fill the air,
With each creak, I feel the flair.
Grandpa's snore, a thunderous boom,
Could wake the flowers in the room.

Pictures hang at odd angles,
Family faces lead to wrangles.
Grandma's recipes, a mystery,
How did she bake that history?

Underneath the dusty shelves,
Lies the chaos of our elves.
They dance and twirl in delight,
Making memories late at night.

Shades of Comfort

In the corner, an old recliner,
Squeaks out tunes - a real whiner.
Uncle Fred claims it's a throne,
With cushions turning to his own.

The fridge hums a quirky song,
Though its contents seem all wrong.
Last week's leftovers, a rainbowed sight,
Guess they're left for a food fight.

Socks in the dryer go to dance,
And leave you with one—what a chance!
Each time we search, we start to laugh,
Who needs matching for a bath?

Sunlight spills on faded walls,
Each crack tells tales, in its brawls.
With every spill, a clink or crash,
Memories linger, and we all mash.

Wisps of Candlelight

At dinner, we light the candles,
But they flicker as if to scandals.
The cat jumps up with a leap,
And dreams of flames, oh what a creep!

The aroma, a blend of delight,
But burnt rolls give quite a fright.
Sister sneezes, and we all jump,
The ceiling vibes with each big thump.

Stories told over waxed wings,
Snapping funny, as laughter sings.
Ghosts of meals come back to haunt,
While Grandpa snores – he's quite the font.

In the dim glow of the night,
Dance of shadows, oh what a sight.
In this chaos, we find our spark,
With candlelight, we laugh till dark.

The Mantelpiece of Dreams

On the shelf, a gnome does grin,
With little shoes, tucked under chin.
Grandma claims it's magic, you see,
But mostly it just looks like me.

Photos placed in no fixed order,
Faces flash like a border.
Uncle Joe with a fish so grand,
Who knew it could sing on command?

Timepieces tick and tock away,
No one cares, it's disarray.
Mom insists they all hold fate,
Yet they only show that we're late.

Under the dust, stories hide,
With memories that gently glide.
Here we gather, a merry crew,
In the oddest moments, dreams come true.

Camellias in the Garden

In the garden, blooms so bright,
Camellias giggle in the light.
They whisper secrets, oh so sly,
As butterflies go floating by.

A rabbit hops, all chubby and round,
In search of snacks that are abound.
He snags a bloom, all pleased and proud,
While flowers laugh, a cheerful crowd.

A squirrel swings, a cheeky chap,
With his bushy tail—a furry flap.
He steals a petal, oh what fun,
In this wild show, he is the one.

So here we laugh, in sunshine's glow,
With silly critters putting on a show.
Every day is a funny spree,
In this garden full of glee.

The Heart that Echoes

In a cozy nook, the echoes play,
A heart that thumps in a funny way.
It trips over socks and coffee mugs,
With giggles shared, and silly hugs.

Pictures hang, they wink and tease,
Captured moments that aim to please.
Each smile caught in a frame so tight,
Turns every day into pure delight.

The clock strikes noon, it's time for lunch,
But first, a dance—oh, what a crunch!
With rhythm gone, we bump and sway,
Our hearts all laughing, come what may.

So here's to joy, and laughter's song,
In every heart, where we belong.
With echoes loud and spirits high,
We'll twirl and spin—oh my, oh my!

Moonlight in the Hall

Under silver beams, the shadows dance,
In the hall where memories prance.
The floorboards creak, they join the fun,
As moonlight winks, a cheeky one.

A cat sneaks by with a dainty paw,
Chasing dust motes—a cheeky draw.
She pounces here, then jumps away,
Making sure she steals the play.

Old clocks chime softly, the hours tease,
As we pull out those ancient keys.
Unlocking giggles from days gone by,
With every laugh, we touch the sky.

So let the moonlight lead the way,
Through echoes of nights, we laugh and sway.
In this hall, where joy stands tall,
Together we shine, never small.

Silhouettes of Us

In the twilight glow, we dance so light,
Silhouettes of us, a funny sight.
With arms like wings, we sway and twirl,
Creating laughter, a joyful whirl.

Every shadow tells a tale,
Of silly moments that never pale.
From everyday quirks to grand delight,
We find the joy in every night.

A noodle fight, or a chase for cake,
Our silhouettes make the ground shake!
With playful dodges and grand displays,
In this wild world, we dance and play.

So raise a toast, to days gone by,
To love and laughter that never die.
In the silhouettes, we stand as one,
Together we spark, forever fun!

Lullabies of Longing

In a room where socks do roam,
The cat pretends she's all alone.
A teddy bear keeps watch at night,
While cookies hide from hungry bites.

Whispers drift through walls so thick,
I swear I heard that clock tick-tick.
Old jokes hang like portraits dear,
Their laughter still echoes near.

The mirror cracks a cheeky grin,
Reflecting tales of where we've been.
Mismatched socks, a funny sight,
Sharing love in silly light.

So here we gather, night or day,
With quirks and giggles in the fray.
For in this haven, hearts all know,
It's laughter that makes love still glow.

Seasons of Embrace

The autumn leaves tumble and twirl,
While grandpa dances, give it a whirl.
Mismatched sweaters, cozy and warm,
Who knew love could take such a form?

Winter brings snowflakes 'round the door,
One snowball fight leads to laughter galore.
Hot cocoa spills in a playful mess,
Yet we all know, it's love, no less.

Springtime blooms with blooms to adore,
The garden gnomes just want to explore.
A picnic gone wrong, with ants in tow,
Reminds us all how fast time can flow.

Summer nights with lightning bugs,
Each one captured with joyful hugs.
In every season, what we see,
It's silly moments that set us free.

The Attic of Reminiscence

Dusty boxes stacked upon a shelf,
Unearthed treasures—it's like finding oneself.
Old clothes from yesteryears lie high,
Will those polka dots still make me sigh?

A bicycle with one wonky wheel,
Reminders of joy that we used to feel.
A record player with some off-tune,
Yet still, it plays our favorite tune.

Ghosts of laughter echo through the beams,
Each vintage find awakens dreams.
A rubber chicken takes the lead,
Who knew nostalgia could be such a need?

In every corner, stories blend,
Time is the laughter that will not end.
So here we sit with hearts so free,
In memories, we find our glee.

Windows to the Soul

Through windows smeared with chocolate smudge,
Peering through the chaos, we won't budge.
The world outside may seem so bright,
But here, we sparkle with laughter's light.

Curtains flutter like playful whims,
As we dance to those old, silly hymns.
A view of cats just plotting schemes,
In this mirth, we're living our dreams.

Sunlight spills like honey, sweet,
Yet socks go missing, each one a cheat.
Laughter flows through every pane,
As shenanigans become our gain.

From this perch, we share our joy,
With every tale of girl and boy.
Windows wide to let love unfold,
In silly smiles, our hearts are told.

Whispers in the Walls

In the corner, the cat sneezes,
While the chair creaks, it pleases.
Messages sent from the chips,
As the wallpaper quietly rips.

A ghost in the attic flies by,
With a broomstick and a pie.
Dishes clatter, a dance of cheer,
While nobody's really here.

Pictures smile from every nook,
Winking secrets like a book.
A sock puppet gives a wink,
As I ponder, what do they think?

Voices echo, a playful shout,
Telling stories, new and out.
Laughter spills from every room,
Creating joy, dispelling gloom.

Echoes of Laughter

The kitchen sings with clattering spoons,
As we mimic our favorite cartoons.
Flipping pancakes, they take flight,
Our breakfast battles, a silly sight.

Socks in the dryer, a game they play,
Once in a while, they slip away.
Racing to find them, we dive and crawl,
In this wild chase, we laugh through it all.

The couch is now a mountain high,
Where explorers gather, reaching the sky.
Pirate ships sail in the bath,
With rubber ducks, we find our path.

Echoes of giggles dance in the halls,
As we hear unexpected falls.
With every stumble, each silly cheer,
We gather memories year after year.

Sheltered in Warmth

A blanket fort, our kingdom grand,
With popcorn scattered across the land.
Teddy bears hold secret courts,
While the dog digs in for snacks, of course.

We sip hot chocolate, marshmallows afloat,
Telling ghost stories that make us gloat.
The lights flicker, a dramatic flair,
As we hide from monsters, giggling with care.

Cousin battles on the video screen,
As we unleash our silly routine.
Dance-offs happen in the hall,
With every slip, we have a ball.

As shadows play with giggles loud,
Our hearts are light, forever proud.
Each moment stacked in layers thick,
Wrapped in warmth, it's magic we pick.

Shadows of Togetherness

In the garden, a race begins,
With hoses spraying and laughter spins.
The dog in mud takes off like a shot,
Leaving a trail that hits the spot.

Under the table, we giggle and hide,
Playing spies with parents inside.
A disaster waiting in the studio,
As paint splatters as we steal the show.

We dive for cover when it rains,
Stomping puddles and making chains.
Each splash a story, a fun retake,
As we fashion boats from leaves we make.

Together we're shadows, laughter loud,
In a wanderlust journey, we're proud.
Through ups and downs, wild and bright,
These moments weave warmth, pure delight.

The Garden of Remembering

In the garden of laughter, we sowed our seeds,
Whispers of giggles echo beneath the trees.
The tomatoes danced, a silly parade,
While squirrels debated, in shades of charade.

Sunflowers winked at our wild, crazy ways,
Bees wearing hats joined in our sunny days.
Birds on the fence shared gossip and tales,
As we giggled at cats who wore funny tails.

In the soil of our joy, memories bloom,
Chasing butterflies, brushing away gloom.
Every toss of confetti, a day well spent,
In our patch of delight, time's magic is lent.

So we'll plant more moments, foster the fun,
With laughter and sunshine, our hearts come undone.
In this plot of remembrance, life's little charms,
Together forever, within nature's arms.

Shadows in the Hallway

In the shadowy hallway, the light plays tricks,
With echoes of laughter, it dances and kicks.
Old photos peek out with a wink and a grin,
In the tales we tell, silliness begins.

The dust bunnies gather for their secret dance,
While socks travel far, look at their chance!
We trip on our memories, giggling with glee,
As we trip over shoes meant for only our feet.

Ghosts of our past wear our favorite hats,
While the clock rolls its eyes at our late-night chitchats.
Every creak of the floorboards keeps up the beat,
And we stumble through times, with love, oh so sweet.

Shadows in hallways hold secrets profound,
In the whispers and chuckles, our joy can be found.
With each step we take, we're writing our tale,
In the house where whimsy and wonders prevail.

Tapestry of Togetherness

In colors of chaos, we weave our delight,
The fabric of memories, stitched tight every night.
With threads of mishaps, our quilt gets so grand,
A tapestry bustling, crafted by hand.

Faded jeans from adventures, unmatched and worn,
Each patch tells a tale, like a child newly born.
In kitchens we gather, with laughter for fuel,
As we bumble through recipes, breaking each rule.

Knitting with humor, and knitting with care,
Every misstep's a grin, a tale that we share.
The stitches of moments, each one is a gleam,
In our quilt of together, we're building a dream.

So we double the yarn and we turn on the charm,
With each loving knot, we keep joy in arm.
For life is a folly, a colorful spree,
In the fabric of friendship, you're fancy, like me!

Footprints in the Dust

Footprints in dust tell a story of fun,
With mischief and mayhem, oh, we're never done.
Each mark is a giggle, a tumble or fall,
A trace of our antics, we've scattered them all.

We dance through the chaos, twirling around,
While dust settles softly, and laughter's the sound.
The vacuum can't handle our flair for the mess,
And we giggle together, no need to impress.

Every scuff on the floor is a memory made,
With socks as our slippers, how silly displayed.
Chasing the giggles, we wander about,
While the dust bunnies cheer us, there's never a doubt.

So leave your footprints, let laughter take flight,
In the dust of our stories, our hearts feel so light.
For here lies the tale of the goofy and spry,
Where silliness echoes beneath every sigh.

Letters Unwritten

In the attic, ghosts still play,
They draft letters but lose their way.
One to Grandma, full of quirks,
But her cat chews it, oh, the perks!

Ink spills here, penguins on parade,
Scribbled messages, plans that fade.
A map to candy, a treasure quest,
But wait, who's hiding? It's the cat, no jest!

Lost sock evidence 'neath the bed,
Each letter reads, 'Check your head!'
Footprints of jelly, laughter and cheer,
In these pages, nothing's severe!

Yet on the fridge, how strong they'd cling,
Note to self: stop doing that thing!
Upcoming pies, and socks quite rare,
Letters unwritten but filled with care.

Songs of Familiar Corners

In the kitchen, pots sing a tune,
A soup opera, oh, how they croon!
Spoons join in with a rhythmic clap,
While flour fights, a messy trap!

The living room echoes with laughter bright,
As cushions plot against the night.
A dance-off starts, no one's in place,
Chasing the dog; oh, what a race!

Upstairs the corners hold secrets tight,
A sock band plays to the moonlight.
Drapes sway, dancing to the beat,
In the hallway, with small, happy feet.

In the study, books lean in close,
Whispering stories, they love the most.
Familiar corners bring joy and song,
In a place where we all belong.

Memories in Every Room

In cozy corners, tales we weave,
With dusty toys that never leave.
A dinosaur roars from under the chair,
While the dog snores as if he can care!

The bathroom's a stage for rubber duck fights,
Where soap suds bubble on whimsical nights.
Toothbrushes dance, a flossing ballet,
Who knew hygiene could lead to such play?

The garage, a hoarder's delight,
With treasures stacked, quite a sight!
Old jigsaw puzzles miss a few parts,
Yet each piece holds familiar hearts.

Every room whispers joy, so bright,
Filling our days, igniting the night.
From toy bins to kitchen tunes' bloom,
There's laughter and love in every room!

Hearth of Heartfelt Echoes

By the fireplace, stories unfold,
Of marshmallow dreams, hot cocoa sold.
A sock now embers, burned in rage,
Who knew socks could steal the stage?

The echo of laughter, a crackling sound,
With family jesters endlessly crowned.
The cat joins in, with a royal flair,
While the dog barks, pretending he's bare!

This hearth of warmth, where we all meet,
With friends, silly dances, and many a treat.
A round of charades, all wildly wrong,
Yet, in these flops, we find where we belong.

In each flicker, a memory's spun,
Through every joke, we come undone.
Heartfelt echoes fill the air,
In life's wild play, a loving affair!

Seasons of Our Being

In spring, we danced, a sneaky twist,
With ice cream sundaes, we couldn't resist.
Summer brought laughter, and water balloon fights,
As we splashed like dolphins on hot sunny nights.

Autumn leaves fell, we dressed as two fools,
Two pumpkins in hats, just breaking the rules.
Winter arrived, and we built a tall snowman,
With a carrot nose and a very bad tan.

Through each season, our silliness grows,
With tickle fights lasting, oh, who really knows?
A home filled with giggles, we'll never outgrow,
Collecting the moments, we're all in the show.

So here's to the seasons, both wild and serene,
Where love's a good joke and laughter's the theme.
In each little corner, each room filled with cheer,
We treasure the whirligigs scattered right here.

The Notebook of Us

In our silly notebook, we scribble and scrawl,
Doodles of inside jokes, we've written them all.
The time you tripped over your own furry shoe,
Or when I mistook the cat for a stew.

Page after page, our memories grow,
From karaoke nights to that time I said 'no'.
We giggle at moments, both silly and bright,
Two lovers still laughing, into the night.

There are lists of our quirks, like who snores the loudest,
And debates about pizza that brought the most proudest.
Each paragraph's scribbled with colors and care,
A testament of love that brings joy everywhere.

So let's keep it going, this hilarious spree,
With doodles and laughter, just you and me.
In our trusty notebook, we pen our delight,
A whimsical record of each grinning bite.

The Love Beneath the Floorboards

Under our floorboards, there's noise and some fun,
Footsteps of laughter, two hearts on the run.
With secrets and shadows, it echoes our glee,
As we dance with the dust bunnies, happy and free.

A squirrel once live-streamed from under our bed,
While we made a sign: 'Do not disturb' -- it said.
Muffled giggles and whispers, a party ensued,
Our floorboards keep secrets, their attitude rude.

Who knew beneath planks, such mischief would thrive,
With a snack supply stash, it feels so alive!
We slip little notes, tucked tight in the seams,
Puns guaranteed to give neighbors wild dreams.

So let's lift the carpet and give a quick peek,
At the silly surprises that hide when we speak.
For our love, dear and mismatched, finds ways to explore,

With jests and puns living beneath every floor.

Chronicles of Laughter

In the chronicles of us, every page makes you grin,
With tales of a cat, who can't quite fit in.
We turn upsidedown, we tackle the mundane,
A simple grocery trip? Oh, what a campaign!

From sock fights at dawn to evening charades,
Our lives filled with laughter, never outshades.
Potato chip dinners and hairbrush fake bands,
We serenade each other, with our unsteady hands.

We've penned down our fumbles and triumphs so bright,
Each day stitched together with giggles outright.
A playlist of moments, we sing out of tune,
Two stepladders waltzing, how do we know the moon?

So join me, dear partner, in our grand jest parade,
With laughter as currency, love can't ever fade.
In this zany book, let's forever embark,
For what's better than laughter? It brightens the dark.

Diary of Moments

In the kitchen, half the cat is found,
Flour on noses, giggles abound.
Eggs on the floor, pancakes in the air,
Breakfast for dinner? Who would dare!

Socks on the ceiling, what a sight!
The dog's wearing one; oh, what a fright!
Toys in the fridge, snacks in the bin,
Laughter erupts, let the chaos begin!

Uncle Joe's snoring, what a delight,
Only to wake when the cake takes flight.
A dance party starts with just one sock,
Mom says, "Shh! When did the door lock?"

We freeze like statues when Dad walks in,
With a grin so wide, it's clear we win.
A diary of moments, we list the fun,
Memories tangled, oh what a run!

Family Ties and Tendrils

A tangled mess of cables and shoes,
Boys in the backyard, singing the blues.
A swing's been made from an old garden chair,
Mom yells, "Stop! Just be aware!"

Grandpa's in the hammock, napping away,
While Grandma's sneakily listing our pay.
"Who'll wash the dog? Not me!" they declare,
But the dog just smiles, he's aware of the snare.

Silly hats worn, mismatched so grand,
Who would've thought this was all planned?
Family ties that twist and twine,
Each day's a joke, a moment divine!

Naps on the sofa, popcorn in bowls,
Finding old treasures, like lost little souls.
Let's keep this chaos, these stories to share,
Oh, how we love this beautiful affair!

Candles in the Twilight

Candles flicker, dance and sway,
While Dad performs his magic ballet.
Dinner rolls fly, who can catch?
As Mom eyes us, with her kitchen batch.

Whispers of shadows, giggles so bright,
The cats play tag in the fading light.
Siblings pretend to be sneaky spies,
While Grandma chuckles, oh what a surprise!

Twilight tales of silly mishaps,
A treasure map drawn on napkin scraps.
Where to stash cookies? A family feat,
Locked in the cupboard where they can't be beat!

Candles melt down, wax on the floor,
While laughter echoes, who could want more?
In these moments, so splendid and sweet,
We gather love, oh isn't life neat?

Chasing Echoes

In the backyard, echoes of squeals,
Are chased by shadows, oh what great deals!
A kite goes high, a dog takes flight,
While Dad chases bubbles with all of his might.

Soda spills over from laughter so loud,
As secrets are shared, this motley crew proud.
The frisbee's now stuck in a tree,
Mom shouts, "Don't cry! We have more than three!"

Chasing echoes that bounce off the wall,
Every corner holds a story or call.
The porch swing creaks, with all of its tales,
While Grandma tells stories of old winds and sails.

Oh, chasing these echoes is never a bore,
Full of surprises and laughter galore.
The air is thick with memories bright,
Each echo a joy, a relentless delight!

Walls That Listen

Walls whisper secrets, oh what a tale,
A cat and a mouse duo never so frail.
They shimmy and shake, causing quite the ruckus,
Who knew a simple house could hold so much fuss?

In the kitchen, the fridge hums a tune so sweet,
While the dog in the corner dreams of feet.
He barks at the shadows, thinks they're a guest,
But only the pots and pans know him best.

Laughter spills out when we dance on the floor,
With socks made of mismatches, we trip and we roar.
The echoing giggles bounce off every wall,
In this lively abode, we're the life of the hall.

So here's to the spaces, both big and quite small,
Where voices can mingle like leaves in the fall.
Each corner's a keeper of jokes and delight,
In this marvelous chaos, everything feels right.

The Rooms We Grew

In the living room, we built a fort so wide,
Pillows for towers, imagination our guide.
Dad thought it was mess, but we said it's a dream,
With snacks in our pockets, we ruled like a team.

The hallway's a runway for our fashion parade,
Socks on our ears, our best clothes displayed.
Mom laughs at our charm, but we strut like stars,
Creating a world that is truly ours.

In the garden, we dug for treasures unknown,
Found a rusty old toy and called it our own.
With dirt on our faces, we shouted with glee,
Every plant held a secret, just waiting for me.

So here's to the rooms where we played and we fought,
The memories linger, though chaos was wrought.
Each wall holds a chuckle, each room tells a tale,
In this quirky castle, we'll always prevail.

Clouds Through the Skylight

We gaze at the clouds through the skylight above,
Each shape brings a giggle—it's what we love.
A dinosaur fighting a fluffy old cat,
What fun we have battling clouds as they chat!

The rain pitter-patters, our own little band,
While we jump in the puddles, all muddy and grand.
Mom yells from the kitchen, 'You'll ruin those shoes!'
But laughter escapes, it's a battle we choose.

Later we'll argue 'bout what's for dessert,
Chocolate or vanilla? It seems life's expert.
With spoons as our swords, a food fight ensues,
We clean up the mess, it's the rules that we choose.

So here's to the days when the sun's shining bright,
When laughter drifts gently, like day turns to night.
The clouds tell our stories, soft whispers of cheer,
In this world of pure joy, we hold each day dear.

Candles and Memories

In the evening glow, we light candles for fun,
A dance party starts, and it's just begun.
The flicker of flames sparks wild charades,
With laughter and love, our energy cascades.

Stories of old weave through the warm air,
Like Grandma's mishap with a very large bear.
Why she thought it was friendly, we'll never quite know,
But we roll on the floor, letting laughter flow.

The wax drips along, as we bust out our moves,
Each twirl is a memory that simply improves.
Silly faces, strange songs, oh what a delight,
This dance in the ambiance feels perfectly right.

So here's to the nights when the candles burn low,
Where memories flicker in the soft golden glow.
With each little flame, more laughter ignites,
This candlelit magic, our hearts take to flights.

The Nooks We Cherish

In cozy corners, laughter flies,
With socks on the ceiling, we reach for the skies.
A cat named Whiskers, on a chair so grand,
Inspects our snacks like she rules the land.

In the pantry, cookies in a heated debate,
While the dog counts seconds, he's starting to wait.
Grandma's old chair, it squeaks with a sigh,
As if it's a witness to pie fights gone by.

We jump on the couch, a trampoline act,
Spilling our dreams, and some juice, that's a fact.
With hidden treasures in every drawer,
Things we forget, but always adore.

So here's to the nooks, where giggles ignite,
And the memories we make, oh what a sight!
In every odd spot, we find our delight,
A sprinkle of joy on a heartwarming night.

Scent of Old Pages

In dusty tomes, we unearth the laughs,
Where characters whisper their quirky gaffes.
Each turn of a page, a tickle and tease,
A comedy sketch, with twists that appease.

With bookmarks of pizza, and notes from our hearts,
We plot out our futures while eating our tarts.
The stories of ghosts that forgot how to scare,
Bump into pranks and a sticky form of air.

A letter from Grandma, all crumpled and torn,
But it tells of her youth, oh the pranks she'd adorn!
A stinky old sock that once danced with flair,
Is lost in a book titled "How Not to Care."

The scent of the pages, like cookies from dreams,
Invites us to giggle, fill life's little seams.
In each laugh and mishap, we find what we seek,
The joy of old stories, from retro to chic.

Lullabies of the Past

The old guitar hums a tune so sweet,
As Dad plays a song with a shaky heartbeat.
While Mom tries to dance, she trips on the rug,
In our laughter, the room feels snug as a bug.

The clock ticks in rhythm, time bends with the song,
As we sing about places where all things go wrong.
Like that time we lost dinner in the yard's tall grass,
And ended up snacking on leftover sass.

A choir of giggles in lullabies weave,
While visiting ghosts take their turn to believe.
Each verse is a treasure, each chorus a hoot,
As the night wraps us tight, in pajama-clad loot.

So here's to the nights filled with whims and with cheer,
Where dreams intertwine with our whispers sincere.
In the lullabies sung, we find our reprise,
In the laughter of memories, we find our sweet sighs.

Dreams Beneath the Roof

Beneath our wild roof, a circus unfolds,
With a trampoline cat and a puppy with gold.
We leap over pillows, in a world turned askew,
Where dreams turn to plans, and grand ideas brew.

The spoon becomes magic, stirring up glee,
As we bake chocolate cookies, all messy and free.
With flour on faces and giggles in tow,
We've crafted a mess that is snack time aglow.

In the attic, adventures lay waiting so bright,
With capes made of sheets, we take off in flight.
The echoes of laughter, they dance through the halls,
As the walls hold our secrets, our stumbles, and falls.

So dreams beneath this roof, we keep them alive,
In every odd moment, where joy seems to thrive.
With a sprinkle of chaos, and stories we weave,
In the tapestry of whimsy, we forever believe.

Heartstrings Woven

In the attic, old shoes abound,
With stories of trips we never found.
A cat wearing socks, oh what a sight,
Chasing dust bunnies, a hilarious plight.

Grandma's old piano plays a tone,
Notes that sound like a dog with a bone.
We dance like fools with missteps and grins,
Our laughter erupts like a soda that spins.

A clock that's stuck at half-past four,
Reminds us of naps on the bedroom floor.
We trip on the rug, then laugh till we weep,
Making memories to hold and to keep.

Under bright stars, we weave silly tales,
Of mishaps with fish and running with snails.
In this quirky space, joy fills the air,
And humor we share beyond all compare.

Portraits of Us

On the wall hangs a portrait of glee,
A family reunion, oh dear, look at me!
With braces and glasses, the values are true,
Captured forever, in a glance, there's you.

Mom tried to bake but the cake took a flight,
Flew right out the window in a most epic fright.
The cat, ever clever, scored quite a bite,
Snagged a piece of frosting, oh what a night!

Dad's epic mustache from the eighties shines bright,
It's a treasure of laughs that brings pure delight.
All these moments, artwork we made,
In laughter's museum, together we stayed.

We gather for stories, each one a delight,
As the past dances back, a warm, goofy sight.
With portraits of us and our laughter-filled spree,
Our hearts are the canvas—brimming with glee.

Stained Glass Dreams

With sunlight spilling in through colored panes,
Our shadows do tango, without any reins.
Grandpa's old jokes, a colorful blend,
Of cracked ribs and chuckles, with no end.

The kitchen a circus, the blender's a roar,
Creating smoothies that spill on the floor.
A dance party starts, with socks all a-spin,
As the dog leaps around, hoping to win.

Chipped mugs holding memories of cheer,
Each sip a reminder that we're all near.
Through stained glass dreams, we take center stage,
A family that laughs at life's every page.

In this space where our laughter is grand,
We paint sunny memories with a slapstick hand.
Together we venture, paint colors so bright,
In our stained glass dreams, everything feels right.

Footsteps on Soft Floors

Every morning echoes with a familiar beat,
Little feet race for breakfast to greet.
A cereal fountain, milk splashing around,
And laughter erupts, an unplanned sound.

The hallway, a runway for high-flying leaps,
As pillows become clouds and laughter creeps.
Slides made of blankets, with giggles galore,
Oh, how we love our soft, creaky floors!

At times we march, on a mission, so grand,
With spoons in our hands like a drummer's command.
But the sheepdog joins in with a wagging tail,
A furry commander, on our bumpy trail.

With every soft footstep, stories unfold,
From tickle fights wild to the secrets we've told.
In this home filled with joy, so vibrant and warm,
Footsteps on soft floors become a sweet charm.

Hallways of Happiness

In the hall with mismatched shoes,
I trip on laughter, sing the blues.
Pictures smile in crooked frames,
While the cat plots her little games.

Socks hide in nooks, a secret stash,
Of silly moments, gone in a flash.
Chasing ghosts with feather dust,
In every corner, a joyful gust.

Jokes etched deep in the wallpaper,
Whispers of fondness, nothing draper.
The echoes of socks, a prankster's delight,
In the whirl of the day and the cozy night.

Upside-down smiles, the walls are spry,
With tales of spills and fun to try.
An empty tub, a rubber duck,
Each splish and splash—oh, what luck!

Secrets Beneath the Staircase

Under the stairs, a world so small,
With a dust bunny kingdom and laughter's call.
Forgotten toys and candy wrappers,
A treasure trove of giggles, none the dapper.

Squeaky steps tell tales so spry,
Of mishaps and mischief, oh my, oh my!
A little mouse with a dance so grand,
Twists and twirls, a tiny band.

Secret snacks hidden in a shoe,
A secret hideout for me and you.
Sunshine whispers in the darkened space,
While shadows twirl in a silly race.

Each creak brings a giggle, a hearty cheer,
As we dive into memories, so crystal clear.
Beneath the stairs, the world is bright,
In every laugh, we find our light.

Medleys of Mementos

A fridge adorned with crayon art,
Of childhood dreams and a dog named Bart.
Half-formed faces, a rainbow's run,
Each odd creation brings out the fun.

From coffee stains to cookie crumbs,
The essence of home, it sweetly hums.
A jar of buttons, a master plan,
To build a spaceship, yes, we can!

Old concert tickets and candy keys,
Dance together like swaying trees.
Each trinket tells a silly tale,
Of laundry days and pets that sail.

With songs of laughter, our hearts take flight,
In the medley of moments, oh what a sight!
Every knickknack, a story spun,
In the waltz of life, we're never done!

The Scent of Home

The smell of bread, a croissant in flight,
Dancing through hallways, a marvelous sight.
With burnt toast battles, the kitchen's alive,
As spices tango, the flavors dive.

A whiff of crayons, a painter's spree,
Fills the air with giggles, can't you see?
Jelly on fingers, a sticky delight,
In the culinary circus, we take to flight.

The aroma of chaos, a chaotic bliss,
Of happy accidents we wouldn't miss.
Each dish a canvas for laughter and cheer,
A symphony sizzling, we hold it dear.

Scented memories, as sweet as pie,
Wrap us in warmth, like a joyful sigh.
The essence of life, so rich, so grand,
In every corner, we lovingly stand.

Hearthside Conversations

In the corner, Aunt Mabel sighs,
While dog jumps up, and cat just lies.
We share our tales, some old, some new,
And laugh until we forget the brew.

Grandpa's snoring beats the stove's warm hum,
While cookies burn, oh what a scrum!
The walls can't hold the glee we make,
With every joke, our hearts, they quake.

The kids all plot to sneak some treats,
While Uncle Joe pretends to cheat.
A game of charades erupts in glee,
As we all dance, and spill our tea.

But in the end, when all is done,
We hug and laugh, our hearts are spun.
In this old haunt, with love we blend,
Our silly moments never end.

Tides of Time

Sandwich crumbs upon the floor,
What was lunch? We can't keep score.
Little ones giggle, chasing the cat,
While Grandpa's hat is squished flat!

The clock chimes loud, but we don't care,
A game of hide and seek, everywhere.
Laughter rolls like waves on the shore,
As we tumble in, wanting more.

Uncle Fred tries to swim in shoes,
While Aunt May plays a joke and snooze.
We make a mess, but that's just fine,
Life's little blunders turn to wine.

Each tide brings new joys to our lives,
While the moon and stars begin their dives.
With each fading splash, we raise a cheer,
For all the fun round here, oh dear!

Stories Beneath the Roof

Beneath this roof, tales take flight,
Like balloons lost on a summer night.
A squirrel named Gerald and his great feat,
Turns into a legend that can't be beat.

Dad claims he once caught a fish that size,
While we all giggle, it's no surprise.
Mom's famous brownies, a heavenly bite,
She says, "It's my secret, not just a rite!"

Whispers echo in this rustic nook,
"Did we ever see that ghost in the book?"
Turns out it's just old Gramps in disguise,
With sheets and laughter, oh what a rise!

The night rolls on with stories galore,
Each twist makes us laugh even more.
With every memory draped in cheer,
We hold dear the warmth that draws us near.

The Table Set with Memories

Our table's set, but where's the pie?
Did Timmy eat it? Oh my, oh my!
Trampling feet beneath our cheer,
There's always chaos when all are here.

The roast chicken's gone, I swear it's true,
While Grandma cackles, we've just one stew.
The juice flows freely, spills on the floor,
Excitement fills every plate, and more!

We toast with plastic cups, all in a row,
Uncle Bill's stories steal the show.
"Remember that time?" echoes around,
As we fall off chairs, laughter unbound.

At the end of the feast, we sigh with glee,
For every moment shared, that's the key.
With crumbs and laughter scattered wide,
Our hearts are full; they swell with pride.

Threads Woven in Time

In the attic, dust bunnies roam,
With ghosts of socks that once called home.
Grandma's knitting spills on the floor,
Each stitch a tale, who could ask for more?

The cat leaps high, swats the yarn ball,
Whiskers twitch—oh, the bobbins fall!
Laughter echoes in the threaded maze,
Tangled stories of far-off days.

Old curtains wave like flags in the fight,
Against the sun, in the morning light.
A world of patterns, each one unique,
In this patchwork haven, we find our peak.

Together we weave, mischief our scheme,
In a tapestry bright, life's silly dream.
With each winding thread, laughter aligns,
Here in this space, where humor entwines.

Stillness in the Living Room

A sofa stuffed with echoes loud,
Where cushions conspire, an unseen crowd.
Remote controls, like lost treasure maps,
Beneath the cushions, a land full of naps.

The clock ticks slow, it jokes with the wall,
Who'll be the first to answer its call?
A table lamp fights shadows with flair,
While dust bunnies giggle without a care.

Every seat tells stories of chairs well sat,
Where laughter erupted and spilled like a hat.
It's a patch of stillness where giggles reside,
In corners of calm, where memories slide.

So let's gather 'round with our snacks so fine,
Make toast to good times with grape juice and wine.
With a wink and a grin, let the stillness bloom,
In our quirky kingdom, dance around the room.

The Kitchen's Heartbeat

The oven beeps like a chef on stage,
As pots and pans join a noisy rage.
Spices dance in a swirling whiff,
While cookies tease, oh what a gift!

The dog sniffs out crumbs like a sleuth,
While the cat plots to claim the fruit.
Laughter bubbles over like boiling stew,
In this bustling space, dreams come true.

Flour clouds form, a white little mist,
As we twirl and spin, you can't resist.
The blender sings a familiar tune,
Creating chaos beneath the moon.

With each sliced onion, a tear may fall,
But who could care with laughter so tall?
This kitchen is life, where fun stirs the pot,
In savory sweetness, we've found our spot.

Unfolding Old Maps

Maps sprawled wide like a puzzle unsolved,
With X marks the spot, all mysteries involved.
Where the dragon lay and pirates would swear,
To treasure chests hidden in playful despair.

We trace the routes with fingers so bold,
Through jungles of laughter and stories retold.
Every wrinkle a journey, every tear a laugh,
Navigating chaos while sipping on half.

The lost coastline of missing socks,
A mountain of books, a sea of clocks.
"Oh look!" I shout, "A land of lost spoons!"
It's an adventure beneath laughing moons.

So let's chart these seas in our quirky way,
Drawing lines of fun from night until day.
With hearts as our compass, we sail on this quest,
In a world of giggles, we find our best.

Pages of Our Story

In the attic, treasures lay,
Where socks and secrets love to play.
A cat that prowls with stealthy grace,
Found grandma's wig in a silly place.

The fridge contains a moldy cheese,
Each bite brings laughter, if you please.
Pancakes flip with extra flair,
As syrup drips, we giggle and stare.

Old letters scribbled with delight,
Reveal our quirks, each Friday night.
The vase of pens held in a rush,
Sometimes they write, but mostly, they're mush.

In corners dark, old tales are spun,
Of dress-up parties, oh, what fun!
From every room, a voice will chirp,
"Remember when?!" as we all burp.

Flickers of Yesterday's Joy

Balloons perched on the ceiling high,
Remind us of the goofy pie.
With cakes that leaned and candles bright,
"Is it the cake or is it the light?"

A rubber chicken at the door,
Squeezed in laughter, begging for more.
Beneath the couch, a treasure found,
A stash of giggles all around.

The old record spins a silly beat,
While dancing feet can't find the street.
We whirl and twirl with youthful grace,
As grandpa's shoes bounce out of place.

The photo wall with funny faces,
Captures moments, silly races.
Each snapshot tells a tale so bold,
Reminders of warm hearts to hold.

Rhythms of Renewal

In the garden, flowers sprout,
But weeds stick up their heads with doubt.
A gnome that grins, a frog that croaks,
We tend our dreams with silly jokes.

The paint peels in a circus hue,
As laughter echoes through the blue.
With each brush stroke, our chaos blooms,
And fills our lives with joyful room.

Windows cracked to let in the sun,
Where shadows play and giggle, run.
The deck chair squeaks a cheery tune,
And sings along with the morning moon.

Each morning greets with cereal fun,
As spoons do battle and toast is won.
Together we rise, with smiles so wide,
A symphony of joy and pride.

Lanterns in the Hall

Lanterns flicker with tales to share,
Of epic fails and funny hair.
As shadows dance across the wall,
Each tale we tell begins a brawl.

A suitcase filled with mismatched shoes,
Invite the feet that refuse to choose.
In every corner, laughter hides,
As socks conspire in silly rides.

The echo of a playful shout,
"Who wore the hat that makes us doubt?"
With every chuckle, mishaps flow,
In darkened halls where memories grow.

The old piano hits a flat,
As pets join in, how about that?
With lanterns bright, love calls us home,
In every corner, we gladly roam.

Hearthstone Heartbeats

In the kitchen, a cat takes a nap,
While we're searching for the last piece of crap.
Mom's recipe's missing, oh what a plight,
Using old socks just to serve up tonight.

Dad's snoring's a soundtrack, we laugh and we tease,
As we swap out the stories like ants with their cheese.
Grandma's old chair creaks, like it's telling a tale,
Of when she once danced with a man named Dale.

We've got mismatched socks hung out for delight,
A fashion so funky, not a chance it's polite.
Will the neighbors complain? We think it's a joke,
Life here's like sweet tea: down-home and bespoke.

Each laughter then echoes through the painted gray walls,

In this space where the chaos so cheerfully sprawls.
For even in madness, love finds a way,
Here's to odd moments we live every day.

Where Time Stands Still

A tick-tock relation with clocks on the shelf,
They giggle and whisper, "Why not just be ourselves?"
So we gather in corners, creased books on our knees,
While the wallpaper peels, laughing back in the breeze.

Pasta gets tossed as the kids break into song,
While Aunt May's cat ambles along, looking wrong.
We don't need a timeline, we've got silly charts,
Fishing for giggles, and catching warm hearts.

If the sun's gone awry, we just light up the night,
With fireflies buzzing and twinkling so bright.
Granddad's old stories go round like a wheel,
Spinning each moment like it's a big deal.

We toast with our glasses, to blunders and falls,
In a world that spins 'round, love hangs on the walls.
Time's a mere player here, just waiting our call,
In this foolish retreat we've designed for us all.

Windows to Our Souls

Our curtains do flutters, a curious cat,
Peeking at neighbors, then giving a pat.
Each window a mirror reflecting the day,
Where the sun hugs our smiles, and troubles just sway.

Laughter bursts forth from pots on the stove,
With soup stirred by folks who just love to rove.
Splatters of sauce on the ceiling lay claim,
To dinner disasters, yet we'll eat just the same.

A knock at the door brings a funny surprise,
With friends dressed as penguins, all wearing ties.
They waltz through the hallway, they trip on the rug,
In this crazy life, there's warmth to hug snug.

So let the world be, just we'll gawk and cheer,
Our windows wide open, inviting all here.
It's a funny ol' dance we do every day,
In our home of delight, where silliness plays.

Fragments of Light

Sunbeams bouncing like kids in a park,
Chasing shadows and giggles, igniting a spark.
We paint all the walls with colors so bright,
Creating a canvas of laughter and light.

From the attic comes down a treasure chest,
Filled with old photos, and we're feeling blessed.
Each snapshot a moment, a tale to unfold,
Like Grandma trying TikTok - oh, that's pure gold.

In the garden we plant our dreams and our hopes,
With weeds that look far too much like small ropes.
As we reminisce past the old garden gate,
Life's a grand adventure, it's never too late.

So we gather the fragments, share stories with flair,
Building memories up like a sack made of air.
In this home of our making, we flourish and strive,
Where joy dances around, and love feels alive.

The Garden of Yesterdays

In the garden where we played,
With flowers that just wouldn't fade.
A gnome that danced, a squirrel in hats,
Chasing tales of runaway cats.

The swings would squeak with every swing,
As laughter soared on butterfly wings.
We'd argue which cloud looked like cheese,
While ants conspired beneath the trees.

With every picnic, crumbs galore,
We'd give them to birds, oh what a score!
The sun would set in a golden flair,
But not before we played truth or dare.

Now I tend to that garden still,
With memories that time can't kill.
Every weed's a story, every thorn's a joke,
In the soil lies laughter—no sign of smoke.

Fireside Stories

By the glow of the embers so bright,
Uncle Bob tells tales that take flight.
With marshmallows roasted to gooey delight,
We giggle as sparks take their flight.

A bear that danced, a cat that could sing,
His stories are wild, like a wind-up spring.
The dog listens close, but can't quite believe,
As shadows of giggles begin to weave.

Grandma's snoring makes quite the sound,
While we sneak cookies that she's tightly wound.
With every crackle, a memory spins,
In a whirlwind of laughter, where fun never thins.

As the fire dims, we'll recall each jest,
These fireside moments we cherish the best.
With a wink and a smile, our hearts a-brim,
Caught in the glow, the world feels so dim.

Paintings of Affection

On canvas bright, our family's art,
Crayon scribbles from each loving heart.
A dog with eight legs, a fish on a bike,
Abstract joy in every stroke, we strike!

Mom paints the sun with a frown and a hat,
While Dad's masterpiece looks more like a cat.
The fridge is our gallery, you'd love it, indeed,
With magnets that hold our colorful creed.

Sister's rainbow runs right off the page,
While brother's creations engage in a rage.
A dance of colors, a whimsical scene,
Where laughter is splattered, and memories glean.

In every artwork, a story unfurls,
Of laughter and doodles in swirling swirls.
With brushes of chaos, our family thrives,
In this vibrant museum, our spirit survives.

Where Time Stands Still

In a room where the clocks have forgotten to tick,
We've snuck in ice cream, oh what a trick!
The couch is our ship, the blanket our sail,
With adventures galore beyond the pale.

The laughter echoes of times gone by,
As we build forts that reach for the sky.
A treasure hunt starts with a sock and a shoe,
Who knew such gems could be found in our view?

The tick-tock of life feels like a parade,
As we twirl in our clothes that the dog just dismayed.
A juggling act with cookies in hand,
While time takes a break, as we laugh on command.

So here in this haven, let the world swirl past,
In this playful realm, our joys hold fast.
With popcorn and giggles, we dance like a thrill,
In moments unmeasured, where time stands still.

www.ingramcontent.com/pod-product-compliance
Lightning Source LLC
Chambersburg PA
CBHW070313120526
44590CB00017B/2664